the guide to owning a
Pomeranian

Vikki Ellmann

T.F.H. Publications, Inc.
One TFH Plaza
Third and Union Avenues
Neptune City, NJ 07753

This book has been published with the intent to provide accurate and authoritative information in regard to the subject matter within. While every precaution has been taken in preparation of this book, the publisher and author assume no responsibility for errors or omissions. Neither is any liability assumed for damages resulting from the use of the information herein.

ISBN 0-7938-1874-5

www.tfh.com

Contents

The History of The Pomeranian

Many authors have tried to link the Pomeranian with ancient dogs in Egypt, Greece and China and have used as evidence the many paintings these civilizations produced. But most dog historians are of the opinion that the Pomeranian was developed from a northern type of dog, such as can still be seen in Iceland and Lapland hauling sleds over the snowy wastelands. And the Pom, despite its diminutive size, still

The Pomeranian's thick coat is a good indication that its origins are from a cold climate area such as Iceland or Lapland, although some believe it to have origins in Egypt, Greece and China.

The Toy Spitz is a Pomeranian of another name. In European countries, the Pomeranian is not recognized because of the presence of the German Spitz.

retains the hardy disposition and thick coat so typical of dogs in cold climates.

There are a number of dogs developed in Central Europe during the middle of the 19th century that are similar in markings and physical appearance to the Pom. The Pom, to many people, is a small Spitz. The Spitz, not recognized by the American Kennel Club (AKC), has many relatives among the purebred dogs of today. Perhaps the closest are the Samoyed and American Eskimo Dog. Also related are the Norwegian Elkhound, the Schipperke, the Keeshond, Volpino Italiano and German Spitzen. In France a similar dog is called the Loulou. In Russia, dogs of the Spitz group are called laikas.

The whole Spitz group is traceable to the dogs of Iceland and Lapland. Whether or not these dogs all had a common ancestor is not known, but there is some speculation that these dogs migrated from northern European areas, such as Finland and Siberia, where they were extremely useful in the cold and desolate areas.

Wurttemberg, the heartland of German dog development, is considered by some as the place where the Spitz was transformed into the Pom. Others believe that the Pomeranian was first developed in the district of Pomerania, where a group of Finns settled in Samogitia.

These first Poms weighed about 30 pounds. They were not nearly as small

Spitz dogs, like the ones seen here, are a cold weather breed. Because of their similarity to Pomeranians, experts have tied the Pom's origins to cold regions.

THE GUIDE TO OWNING A POMERANIAN

as today's Pom, but they were definitely considered small dogs. The colors were mostly white, cream or black. It is thought that German breeders wished to obtain a smaller dog than the prevailing Spitz or Samoyed and bred the dog down in size.

THE POMERANIAN IN ENGLAND

While we give the Germans credit for their role in producing these tiny dogs, the Pom really came into its own in England. Queen Victoria is known for many things, but in the dog world she is given special credit for bringing the popularity of the Pomeranian to a peak. While the Pom or a near ancestor is thought to have been in England since before 1800, the Queen was greatly pleased by a tiny Pom named Marco while she was vacationing in Florence, Italy, and she brought him home to the British public. She exhibited many Poms and won with some of them, one of her most famous being Windsor's Marco. It is said that when the Queen was dying, she asked that her favorite dogs be admitted to the sickroom so she might play with them.

In 1870, the Pomeranian was recognized by the English Kennel Club and there were three entries in 1871 at one of the big dog shows. The Pom Club was founded in 1871, and one of the earliest enthusiasts was Miss Lilla Ives, who imported many Poms from Germany. It is interesting to note, in a book on

Early Pomeranians were larger than those of today. They were breed down from these larger dogs to become the tiny size we now see.

Poms written early in this century, that the list of Pom breeders was made up almost entirely of women. It would appear that this particular breed was very popular with the ladies and that most of the early kennels were founded by women. It is a credit to their efforts that we have the handsome Pom of today.

These early Pomeranians weighed 20 pounds or more and were mostly black or white in coat color. It was the English breeders who brought the dog down in size and developed the many different colors. They differentiated between very small Poms of less than seven pounds and larger ones over seven pounds.

Some of the famous early English champions were Ch. Sable Mite, Sable Atom and Tina. Another outstanding sire was Little Nipper. Different kennels became noted for different types of Poms. One, for example, was known for creams and whites.

Among the famous authors and painters who loved the Pom is Ouida, the English author who wrote of "Ruffino," a tiny Pomeranian dog. Gainesborough, a painter, also pictured a small toy much like our Pom, although he predates the official entry of the Pomeranian into England.

THE POMERANIAN IN AMERICA

Poms were brought to America from England, rather than from the Continent. The first Pom to be shown was Sheffield Lad, who was exhibited in 1892. You can imagine the excitement these tiny dogs caused with their beautiful coats and bouncy, playful manner. The breed was not recognized by the AKC, however, until 1900, the same year the American Pomeranian Club was founded.

At first the Pom was exhibited in the Miscellaneous Class, but he was soon moved to the Toy Group. There Nubian Rebel won Best of Breed in 1900. The breed rapidly grew in popularity as people discovered the ease of care and pleasure these little dogs afforded them, and by 1911 there were enough Pom breeders and owners to hold a specialty show. The winner was Ch. Banner Prince.

At this time the show classes included separate classes for weight: under seven and over seven pounds. In these early days, there were four popular colors of Poms: white, black, chocolate and blue (a difficult color to breed and maintain). Some of the outstanding champions were Dainty Mite, Princess Hula, who was famous as a brood bitch as well as a show champion, and Twilight, the sire of many champions.

BREED DEVELOPMENT

Many breeds of dogs didn't just grow. Dog owners and breeders

The Pomeranian's diminutive size, attractive coat, and intelligent disposition make him an excellent companion.

wanted certain types of dogs for special purposes and, because of this desire, encouraged purebreds. In the case of the Pomeranian, we know that its ancestors were the sled dogs of the North. These dogs migrated across Northern Europe into Central Europe, where the Germans bred them. The heavy double coat was retained when the dogs became household pets. Although they no longer were obliged to tow boats along the canals or pull sleds in cold climates, their coats were so attractive that breeders spent much effort to improve the quality and coloration. Because the Pom was essentially a pet, not a working breed, the niceties of appearance were (and are) important.

The Germans, perhaps wanting a smaller dog suitable for city living, bred the original Spitz down in size. These dogs were still 20 pounds and over when they reached England's shores. The English, enchanted by these small but bouncy dogs, bred them still smaller in size. This was probably done by mating the smallest dogs (which still maintained the best characteristics of the breed) they could find, so that the puppies of resulting litters were smaller than average.

Selective breeding achieved the tiny size of today's Pom. Selective breeding is still being continued in the United States, and it was noted in the *Pomeranian Review* in September 1961 that judges seemed to want smaller dogs, with the trend toward shorter, blunter heads. There are disadvantages in smallness, as most veterinarians will tell you, so breeders must exercise care not to make such body changes that may encumber reproduction. Many breeders prefer to breed their larger bitches for this reason.

Early breeders also noted other factors when breeding their Poms. They saw that certain colors, such as the blues, were hard to maintain. They found, by experiment, that whites did not breed as small as other colors, that certain coat colors meant better or poorer coats. Trial and error, plus knowledge of Mendelian genetic theories, aided the breeders in their work.

Toy dogs have always been household pets. While their yapping can frighten off unwelcome intruders, we doubt that they can do much physical damage. Although there are stories of Poms being successfully used as ratters, there seems to be little call for this skill these days. History has bred into these dogs a diminutive size, attractive coat and an intelligent disposition to make the Pom a true companion.

The Standard for the Pomeranian

A breed standard is the criterion by which the appearance (and to a certain extent, the temperament as well) of any given dog is made subject to objective measurement. Basically, the standard for any breed is a definition of the perfect dog to which all specimens of the breed are compared. Breed standards are always subject to change through review by the national breed club for each dog, so it is always wise to keep up with developments in a breed by checking the publications of your

Pomeranians are small, alert dogs with well-balanced frames. Royal and wise in appearance, this Pomeranian is a fine example of the breed.

national kennel club. Printed below is the American Kennel Club standard for the Pomeranian.

General Appearance—The Pomeranian in build and appearance is a cobby, balanced, short-coupled dog. He exhibits great intelligence in his expression, and is alert in character and deportment.

Size, Proportion, Substance—*Size*—The weight of the Pomeranian for exhibition is from three to seven pounds. The ideal size for show specimens is four to five pounds. *Proportions*—The Pomeranian in build and appearance is a cobby, balanced, short-coupled dog. The legs are of medium length in proportion to a well balanced frame. *Substance*—The body is well ribbed and rounded. The brisket is fairly deep and not too wide.

Head—*Head* well proportioned to the body, wedged-shaped, with a fox-like expression. *Eyes* bright, dark in color, and medium in size, almond-shaped and not set too wide apart nor close together. Pigmentation around eye rims must be black, except self-colored in brown and blue. *Ears* small, carried erect and mounted high on the head and placed not too far apart.

Skull not domed in outline. A round, domey skull is a *major fault*. *Muzzle*—There is a pronounced *stop* with a rather fine but snipy muzzle. Pigment around lips must be black, except self-colored in brown and blue. *Bite*—The teeth meet in a scissors bite, in

Deep in thought and enjoying the weather, this dog shows the black pigmentation around the eyes and mouth as required by the breed standard.

The head of the Pomeranian is wedge-shaped with a fox-like expression.

which part of the inner surface of the upper teeth meets and engages part of the outer surface of the lower teeth. One tooth out of line does not mean an undershot or overshot mouth. An undershot mouth is a *major fault*.

Neck, Topline, Body—*Neck*—The neck is rather short, its base set well back on the shoulders. *Topline* is level. *Body*—The body is cobby, being well ribbed and rounded. *Chest*—the brisket is fairly deep and not too wide. *Tail*—The tail is characteristic of the breed. It turns over the back and is carried flat, set high.

Forequarters—*Shoulders*—The Pom is not straight in shoulder, but has sufficient layback of shoulders to carry the neck proudly and high. *Forelegs*—The forelegs are straight and parallel, of medium length in proportion to a well balanced frame. *Pasterns*—The Pomeranian stands well up on toes. Down in pasterns is a *major fault*. Dewclaws on the forelegs may be removed. *Feet*—The Pomeranian stands well up on toes.

Hindquarters—*Legs*—The hocks are perpendicular to the ground, parallel to each other from hock to heel, and turning neither in nor out. Cow-hocks or lack of soundness in hind legs or stifles are *major faults*. Dewclaws, if any, on the hind legs are generally removed. *Feet*—The Pomeranian stands well up on toes.

Coat—*Body Coat*—Double-coated: a short, soft, thick undercoat with

A classic example of the Pomeranian's balanced body: straight, parallel legs, laid-back shoulders, turned-up tail, and an up-on-toes stance.

Pure white Pomeranians are an acceptable color to be judged for show.

THE GUIDE TO OWNING A POMERANIAN

longer, coarse, glistening outercoat consisting of guard hairs which must be harsh to the touch in order to give the proper texture for the coat to form a frill of profuse, standing-off straight hair. A soft, flat or open coat is a *major fault*. *Tail Coat*—It is profusely covered with hair. *Leg Coat*—The front legs are well feathered and the hindquarters are clad with long hair or feathering from the top of the rump to the hocks.

Trimming—Trimming for neatness is permissible around the feet and up the back of the legs to the first joint; trimming of unruly hairs on the edges of the ears and around the anus is also permitted. Overtrimming (beyond the location and amount described in the breed standard) should be *heavily penalized*.

Color—*Classifications*—The Open Classes at Specialty shows may be divided by color as follows: Open Red, Orange, Cream & Sable; Open Black, Brown & Blue; Open Any Other Allowed Color.

Acceptable colors to be judged on an equal basis. Any solid color, any solid color with lighter or darker shadings of the same color, any solid color with sable or black shadings, parti-color, sable and black & tan. Black & tan is black with tan or rust, sharply defined, appearing above

The Pomeranian's outer coat consists of guard hairs that are harsh to the touch, giving the proper texture for the coat to form a frill of profuse, standing-off straight hair

each eye and on the muzzle, throat, and forechest, on all legs and feet and below the tail. Parti-color is white with any other color distributed in even patches on the body and a white blaze on the head. A white chest, foot, or leg on a whole-colored dog (except white) is a *major fault*.

Gait—The Pomeranian moves with a smooth, free, but not loose action. He does not elbow out in front nor move excessively wide nor cow-hocked behind. He is sound in action.

Temperament—He exhibits great intelligence in his expression, and is alert in character and deportment.

A Description of the Pomeranian

When you first went dog-hunting, did you know that you wanted a Pomeranian?

Many people see a young puppy, and he is so cute that they immed-iately dash off and purchase one just like him.

Others come to like a dog they see in someone's home and ask where they can purchase a similar one. Or, if

The Pomeranian's diminutive size and light weight make him easy to carry.

The Pomeranian is as comfortable romping around your yard as he is sitting in your lap.

Pomeranians love attention and affection, and they make perfect "lap dogs."

THE GUIDE TO OWNING A POMERANIAN

one of the dogs in the neighborhood has a litter of puppies, you will often find some of her children in nearby homes.

Still others, more scientific in their selection, go to the library and look up different breeds of dogs, or write to the national kennel club for advice and information. Or they may find their dog through the pet magazines in which breeders advertise puppies for sale. Visiting the local dog shows is another excellent way to see the various types of dogs before making a choice.

Your new Pomeranian will have some very special qualities, and you need to know what to expect, temperamentally and physically. The Pomeranian is a toy dog weighing between three and seven pounds, with the average weight being four to five pounds. Despite his small size, the Pom is a hardy little fellow who delights in play and affection. Although children must be careful not to play too roughly with him, they will find that he responds to gentle games and fun. As a house companion the Pom knows no equal, and a pair of Poms will double the fun. His size makes him ideal for apartment dwellers, and while he may not be physically able to rout unwelcome callers, his loud yapping bark may very well ward them off.

One of the Pomeranian's proudest assets is the handsome coat he inherits from his sled-dog ancestors, and breeders have taken great care to encourage this fine coat, as well as to breed the Pomeranian to small size.

The Pomeranian may resemble the fox in expression and color as well as in cunning and intelligence.

TEMPERAMENT

Animal behaviorists are not sure whether certain traits of behavior are inherited or not, but we do know that the best dogs (from a genetic standpoint) can be ruined by improper training and care. And a relatively unpromising dog can certainly become a faithful and loving pet if he is well treated.

The Pom, improperly treated and trained, can develop into a yappy little dog with a tendency to snap, especially at children. In the early days there were some strains which seemed more temperamental than others, but breeders made every effort to breed out this characteristic. Yapping should be curbed and ill-tempered dogs should not be tolerated.

It is a fact, however, that Poms should not be subjected to the onslaught of too many children. This is because children often do not understand how to handle small dogs and sometimes pull the Pom's luxuriant coat or play too roughly.

One of the endearing features of this dog is his frisky, perky attitude. He is indeed a bouncy little dog always willing to follow master or mistress in search of fun. It is a great mistake to get into the habit of making the Pom a lap dog. When walking, he should be on a leash, not held, and at home, he should be allowed freedom and exercise.

In addition to this, the Pom is also very intelligent and trainable. In recent obedience trials, the Pom has been a consistent winner.

APPEARANCE

It often seems to the observer that the Pom is all coat. Indeed, with his outstanding ruff of hair, the fluffy undercoat, little legs and ears appearing out of nowhere, he does look like a little puffball. In recent years the head has become a bit shorter and blunter, but the AKC describes the head as "foxy" in outline. The standard specifies that the Pom should be compact and well-knit in frame. When the judges look over a show dog, they not only note the appearance of the coat but feel the body in order to determine that the frame is also a model of excellence.

When the Pom is walking, he almost seems to bounce off the ground, and while he will take no prizes for the one-minute mile, a properly bred Pom should gait neatly with no evidence of paddling or weaving.

LIFE SPAN

Most Poms live to a ripe old age if given proper care. Some may even reach 18 or 20 years, but 12 to 14 is about average.

Your New Pomeranian Puppy

SELECTION

When you do pick out a Pomeranian puppy as a pet, don't be hasty; the longer you study puppies, the better you will understand them. Make it your transcendent concern to select only one that radiates good health and spirit and is lively on his feet, whose eyes are bright, whose coat shines, and who comes forward eagerly to make and to cultivate your acquaintance. Don't fall for any shy little darling that wants to retreat to his bed or his box, or plays coy behind other puppies or people, or hides his head under your arm or jacket appealing to your protective instinct. *Pick the Pomeranian puppy who forthrightly picks you! The feeling of attraction should be mutual!*

DOCUMENTS

Now, a little paper work is in order.

Picking the perfect puppy is going to take time and patience. Looking at these three, how could anyone decide on just one?

When you purchase a purebred Pomeranian puppy, you should receive a transfer of ownership, registration material, and other "papers" (a list of the immunization shots, if any, the puppy may have been given; a note on whether or not the puppy has been wormed; a diet and feeding schedule to which the puppy is accustomed) and you are welcomed as a fellow owner to a long, pleasant association with a most lovable pet, and more (news)paper work.

GENERAL PREPARATION

You have chosen to own a particular Pomeranian puppy. You have chosen it very carefully over all other breeds and all other puppies. So before you ever get that Pomeranian puppy home, you will have prepared for its arrival by reading everything you can get your hands on having to do with the management of Pomeranians and puppies. True, you will run into many conflicting opinions, but at least you will not be starting "blind." Read, study, digest. Talk over your plans with your veterinarian, other "Pomeranian people," and the seller of your Pomeranian puppy.

When you get your Pomeranian puppy, you will find that your reading and study are far from finished. You've just scratched the surface in your plan to provide the greatest possible comfort and health for your Pomeranian; and, by the same token, you do want to assure yourself of the greatest possible enjoyment of this wonderful creature. You must be

Have safe chew toys, such as those made by Nylabone®, available for your new Pomeranian when he arrives in your home. They will help to keep him occupied.

THE GUIDE TO OWNING A POMERANIAN

As adults, most Pomeranians love to ride in the car, but transportation of your new puppy takes special care so that he doesn't get sick.

ready for this puppy mentally as well as in the physical requirements.

TRANSPORTATION

If you take the puppy home by car, protect him from drafts, particularly in cold weather. Wrapped in a towel and carried in the arms or lap of a passenger, the Pomeranian puppy will usually make the trip without mishap. If the pup starts to drool and to squirm, stop the car for a few minutes. Have newspapers handy in case of car-sickness. A covered carton lined with newspapers or a Nylabone® Fold-Away Pet Carrier will provide protection for puppy and car, if you are driving alone. Avoid

excitement and unnecessary handling of the puppy on arrival. A Pomeranian puppy is a very small "package" to be making a complete change of surroundings and company, and he needs frequent rest and refreshment to renew his vitality.

THE FIRST DAY AND NIGHT

When your Pomeranian puppy arrives in your home, put him down on the floor and don't pick him up again, except when it is absolutely necessary. He is a dog, a real dog, and must not be lugged around like a rag doll. Handle him as little as possible, and permit no one to pick

When you first get your new puppy home, put him down and don't pick him up. Allow him to wander and get accustomed to his surroundings.

him up and baby him. To repeat, *put your Pomeranian puppy on the floor or the ground and let him stay there except when it may be necessary to do otherwise.*

Quite possibly your Pomeranian puppy will be afraid for a while in his new surroundings, without his mother and littermates. Comfort him and reassure him, but don't console him. Don't give him the "oh-you-poor-itsy-bitsy-puppy" treatment. Be calm, friendly, and reassuring. Encourage him to walk around and sniff over his new home. If it's dark, put on the lights. Let him roam for a few minutes while you and everyone else concerned sit quietly or go about your routine business. Let the puppy come back to you.

Playmates may cause an immediate problem if the new Pomeranian puppy is to be greeted by children or other pets. If not, you can skip this subject. The natural affinity between puppies and children calls for some supervision until a live-and-let-live relationship is established. This applies particularly to a Christmas puppy, when there is more excitement than usual and more chance for a puppy to swallow something upsetting. It is a better plan to welcome the puppy several days before or after the holiday week. Like a baby, your Pomeranian puppy needs much

The best companion for a new puppy is another puppy. Due to their small size, it is easy to keep more than one Pom.

The Nylabone® Fold-Away Pet Carrier is a great housetraining tool. Change the puppy's bedding if it becomes dirty or soiled.

rest and should not be over-handled. Once a child realizes that a puppy has "feelings" similar to his own, and can readily be hurt or injured, the opportunities for play and responsibilities provide exercise and training for both.

For his first night with you, he should be put where he is to sleep every night—say in the kitchen, since its floor can usually be easily cleaned. Let him explore the kitchen to his heart's content; close doors to confine him there. Prepare his food and feed him lightly the first night. Give him a pan with some water in it—not a lot, since most puppies will try to drink the whole pan dry. Give him an old coat or shirt to lie on. Since a coat or shirt will be strong in human scent, he will pick it out to lie on, thus furthering his feeling of security in the room where he has just been fed.

HOUSETRAINING HELPS
Now, sooner or later—mostly sooner—your new Pomeranian puppy is going to "puddle" on the floor.

Puppies, like babies, need rest and solitude for a time. Too much excitement early on can frighten a puppy making him slower to bond with his new owners.

Choosing a puppy should be a mutual decision between you and the puppy. The best puppy for you is the one that picks you.

First take a newspaper and lay it on the puddle until the urine is soaked up onto the paper. Save this paper. Now take a cloth with soap and water, wipe up the floor and dry it well. Then take the wet paper and place it on a fairly large square of newspapers in a convenient corner. When cleaning up, always keep a piece of wet paper on top of the others. Every time he wants to "squat," he will seek out this spot and use the papers. (This routine is rarely necessary for more than three days.) Now leave your Pomeranian puppy for the night. Quite probably he will cry and howl a bit; some are more stubborn than others on this matter. But let him stay alone for the night. This may seem harsh treatment, but it is the best procedure in the long run. Just let him cry; he will weary of it sooner or later.

Grooming the Pomeranian

Grooming is a matter of habit for both dog and master. Regular grooming should be a pleasure for both, and it will be if your pet is accustomed to his weekly combing and brushing. Start grooming early, be kind but firm, and you will find that he welcomes his grooming sessions.

Like this dog, your Pomeranian must be taught to be still while you are bathing him. If your dog confuses grooming time with play time...it's going to be a long day.

The Pomeranian's coat is one of the most beautiful of all. A poorly groomed coat is a reflection of the owner not the dog.

TRAINING FOR PLEASURABLE GROOMING

The first thing to teach your dog is *patience* during grooming. Don't allow him to "act up" at this time; after all, who's boss anyway! He must learn to stand quietly while being combed, brushed, or trimmed. If you begin when your puppy is quite small, he will soon learn to enjoy grooming. Some breeders start to brush the puppies while they are still in the nest and have little difficulty later when the puppies grow up.

The easiest place to groom a dog is on a table or bench. Special grooming tables can be purchased. At the start, if your pet is nervous, attach the leash to a hook above the table or bench, which will hold him in place. If your dog is very young or still unsure, start your grooming activities (brushing, combing, etc.) from the rear, so that he becomes accustomed to the sensations gradually.

YOUR POMERANIAN'S COAT

A dog is the direct reflection of his heredity, diet, and general health and is shown to his best by grooming. Proper care of the coat will ensure that it is shiny and free from parasites and skin ailments.

With a thorough drying, this Pomeranian's coat will be as fluffy as ever.

dandruff since the skin continually sheds and renews itself.

Most breeds of dogs have two coats: a soft undercoat and an outer coat. The Pomeranian's coat is his glory, a thick, fluffy undercoat, and a straight harsh outer coat. This coat needs regular care in order to maintain its appearance. Every Pom owner should be prepared to spend the necessary time and effort to keep the coat looking its best.

During the time when your Pom is maturing, his coat will undergo several changes. Some Poms change color (blues often begin as blacks). But in all Poms it takes about one

Once they're used to it, most dogs love a good brushing. Combing the Pom isn't necessary, except to remove matts and burrs.

The skin and coat of all dogs have certain general characteristics in common, regardless of breed. The skin contains oil glands (which secrete oil to keep the coat shiny and waterproof), the sebaceous glands (related to hair growth), and some sweat glands. The sebaceous glands secrete a waxy substance called sebum, which coats the hair as it grows. It is this substance which you will often find coating your dog's collar, and sometimes accounts for that doggy odor. Do not be surprised if your dog occasionally develops

The thick, fluffy coat takes much care. Regular grooming, although time consuming, is necessary to keep your Pom clean and healthy.

year before the full adult coat appears and this coat is not fully developed, often until the dog is three or fours years old.

At two months your dog's coat will be long and fluffy, extending to the point of the ears; at three months, it starts shedding and becoming ragged; and by four or five months, the coat is shed and your dog may have become a short-haired variety. Don't despair: this is only temporary and by ten months the double coat will have developed considerably and be on the way to its full beauty.

COMBING AND BRUSHING

Combing and brushing should be a weekly or even daily event. To keep the coat from matting takes care and patience. Combing is seldom necessary and many owners think it is unnecessary or even bad for the coat. Use the comb only to remove mats or burs. Do not cut out burs, but gently pry them apart using a wide-toothed comb. The comb can also be used for a final touch when you fluff out the leg furnishings and neaten up the hair behind the ears.

Perhaps the most important grooming aid is a proper brush. You can purchase a good bristle brush in any pet store. When brushing the Pom, start from the back and work forward. Lay him on the table and brush the stomach first. Then turn him over and brush the top part of his coat. If you separate the coat into layers you will find that the job is more thorough and you can check for parasites and skin ailments while you are grooming. The tail should be brushed from the roots and the rest of the body brushed downward. At the very end, starting at the back, brush from the tail to the head so that you raise the coat.

NAIL CLIPPING

Long nails can force a dog's toes outward and permanently affect his stance if this occurs during puppyhood. If you enjoy an

When brushing, don't forget to check your dog for parasites and skin ailments. These can be easily missed in a coat as thick as a Pomeranian's.

A weekly brushing, or daily if you're inclined, is necessary to keep the Pomeranian's coat from matting.

occasional romp with your pet, you will also find it safer for both you and your clothing if the nails are kept clipped. As part of your Pom's regular checkup the veterinarian can clip his nails. Ask him to show you how to do this chore so you can do it in the future. If you purchase a good pair of clippers, you can do it yourself. The part you must trim is the hook, the section of the nail which curves downward. Be careful not to cut into the quick, as it bleeds profusely. In small puppies or light-haired dogs, the line where the vein begins is easy to spot. In dark-colored nails this is more difficult to

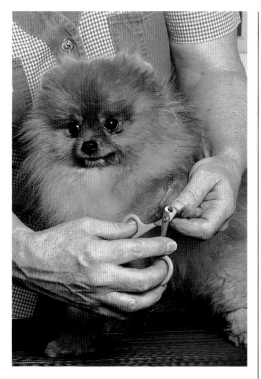

When clipping your Pomeranian's nails, be careful not to cut too much or you will cut the quick.

see, but shining a flashlight under the nail will help you find the quick.

Are you nervous about clipping? Then file the nails. A good wood file can do an excellent job of shortening nails, or you can use the file to finish off the job of clipping. When you first begin to file, you will have to bear down quite hard to break the hard polished surface of the nail. Draw the file in one direction, from the top of the nail downward in a round stroke to the end of the nail.

If you do accidentally cut into the dog's toes, it's not fatal; apply a styptic pencil and bandage the foot until the bleeding has stopped. The bandage will keep the blood from splattering around.

Most people find that their dogs need nail trimming about once every two months. If your dog walks mostly on concrete sidewalks, his nails will wear down naturally and he may never need a clipping.

TRIMMING

The Pomeranian should never be clipped, for clipping changes the color of the coat. But, there is a need for some trimming of straggly hair to keep the coat neat. Trimming should be done on a weekly basis. If you are entering your dog in a show, the coat should be trimmed at least two weeks before the show.

Pomeranian coats need a little trimming every now and then to remove straggly hair and keep the coat looking neat.

The full coat of the Pomeranian takes time to blossom. It usually takes about three to four years to develop completely.

The tail should be scissored for a neat look, but do not trim too closely so that it looks clipped and bare. Lay the tail flat and trim the hair close to the root of the tail. Then trim the hair around the anus.

Pom feet have charm: little cat feet, jutting out from the mass of hair. The paws should be trimmed so that they are free of straggly hair. The area on the sides and back of the legs can also be scissored free of stray hairs.

The next major trimming job is the ears. Again, the ears should appear to spring out from the halo of hair surrounding the head. Trim the inside edge of the ear hair to a quarter-inch-length, and the outside edge to one-half inch. While you are trimming the ears, hold the tip so that you don't cut the skin.

Trimming shears can be obtained in the pet store, but if you are nervous about this task, you can have it done professionally.

Feeding Your Pomeranian

Now let's talk about feeding your Pomeranian, a subject so simple that it's amazing there is so much nonsense and misunderstanding about it. Is it expensive to feed a Pomeranian? No, it is not! You can feed your Pomeranian economically and keep him in perfect shape the year round, or you can feed him expensively. He'll thrive either way, and let's see why this is true.

First of all, remember a Pomeranian is a dog. Dogs do not have a high degree of selectivity in their food, and unless you spoil them with great variety (and possibly turn them into poor, "picky" eaters) they will eat almost anything that they become

Feeding Pomeranians is easy because they are not picky eaters (unless you spoil them). Feeding dogs in a group incites appetite and competition.

This may not be the "good china," but the meal inside is delicious and nutritious.

Hundreds of thousands of dollars have been spent in canine nutrition research. The results are pretty conclusive, so you needn't go into a lot of experimenting with trials of this and that every other week. Research has proven just what your dog needs to eat and to keep healthy.

DOG FOOD

There are almost as many right diets as there are dog experts, but the basic diet most often recommended is one that consists of a dry food, either meal or kibble form. There are several of excellent quality, manufactured by reliable companies, research tested, and nationally advertised. They are inexpensive, highly satisfactory, and easily available in stores everywhere in containers of five to 50 pounds. Larger amounts cost less per pound, usually.

If you have a choice of brands, it is usually safer to choose the better known one; but even so, carefully read the analysis on the package. Do not choose any food in which the protein level is less than 25 percent, and be sure that this protein comes from both animal and vegetable sources. The good dog foods have meat meal, fish meal, liver, and such, plus protein from alfalfa and soy beans, as well as some dried-milk product. Note the vitamin content carefully. See that they are all there in

accustomed to. Many dogs flatly refuse to eat nice, fresh beef. They pick around it and eat everything else. But meat—bah! Why? They aren't accustomed to it! They'd eat rabbit fast enough, but they refuse beef because they aren't used to it.

VARIETY NOT NECESSARY

A good general rule of thumb is forget all human preferences and don't give a thought to variety. Choose the right diet for your Pomeranian and feed it to him day after day, year after year, winter and summer. But what is the right diet?

Your Pomeranian needs fresh, clean water just as much as he needs a healthy, nutritious dog food.

good proportions; and be especially certain that the food contains properly high levels of vitamins A and D, two of the most perishable and important ones. Note the B-complex level, but don't worry about carbohydrate and mineral levels. These substances are plentiful and cheap and not likely to be lacking in a good brand.

The advice given for how to choose a dry food also applies to moist or canned types of dog foods, if you decide to feed one of these.

Having chosen a really good food, feed it to your Pomeranian as the manufacturer directs. And once you've started, stick to it. Never change if you can possibly help it. A switch from one meal or kibble-type food can usually be made without too much upset; however, a change will almost invariably give you (and your Pomeranian) some trouble.

WHEN SUPPLEMENTS ARE NEEDED

Now what about supplements of various kinds, mineral and vitamin, or the various oils? They are all okay to add to your Pomeranian's food. However, if you are feeding your Pomeranian a correct diet, and this is easy to do, no supplements are necessary unless your Pomeranian has been improperly fed, has been sick, or is having puppies. Vitamins and minerals are naturally present in all the foods; and to ensure against any loss through processing, they are added in concentrated form to the dog food you use. Except on the advice of your veterinarian, added amounts of vitamins can prove

Following a good feeding schedule and staying away from too many supplements will help to keep your Pom healthy and active.

THE GUIDE TO OWNING A POMERANIAN

harmful to your Pomeranian! The same risk goes with minerals.

FEEDING SCHEDULE

When and how much food to give your Pomeranian? As to when (except in the instance of puppies), suit yourself. You may feed two meals per day or the same amount in one single feeding, either morning or night. As to how to prepare the food and how much to give, it is generally best to follow the directions on the food package. Your own Pomeranian may want a little more or a little less.

Fresh, cool water should always be available to your Pomeranian. This is important to good health throughout his lifetime.

ALL POMERANIANS NEED TO CHEW

Puppies and young Pomeranians need something with resistance to chew on while their teeth and jaws are developing—for cutting the puppy teeth, to induce growth of the permanent teeth under the puppy teeth, to assist in getting rid of the puppy teeth at the proper time, to help the permanent teeth through the gums, to ensure normal jaw development, and to settle the permanent teeth solidly in the jaws.

The adult Pomeranian's desire to chew stems from the instinct for tooth cleaning, gum massage, and jaw exercise—plus the need for an outlet for periodic doggie tensions.

Safe chew toys, such as those made by Nylabone®, will help keep your Pomeranian busy, as well as keep his teeth clean.

This is why dogs, especially puppies and young dogs, will often destroy property worth hundreds of dollars when their chewing instinct is not diverted from their owner's possessions. And this is why you should provide your Pomeranian with something to chew—something that has the necessary functional qualities, is desirable from the Pomeranian's viewpoint, and is safe for him.

It is very important that your Pomeranian not be permitted to chew on anything he can break or on any indigestible thing from which he can

Chewing is a natural instinct for all dogs. Give him a safe chew toy to play with.

bite sizable chunks. Sharp pieces, such as from a bone which can be broken by a dog, may pierce the intestinal wall and kill. Indigestible things that can be bitten off in chunks, such as from shoes or rubber or plastic toys, may cause an intestinal stoppage (if not regurgitated) and bring painful death, unless surgery is promptly performed.

Strong natural bones, such as 4- to 8-inch lengths of round shin bone from mature beef—either the kind you can get from a butcher or one of the variety available commercially in pet stores—may serve your Pomeranian's teething needs if his mouth is large enough to handle them effectively. You may be tempted to give your Pomeranian puppy a smaller bone and he may not be able to break it when you do, but puppies grow rapidly and the power of their jaws constantly increases until maturity. This means that a growing Pomeranian may break one of the smaller bones at any time, swallow the pieces, and die painfully before you realize what is wrong.

All hard natural bones are very abrasive. If your Pomeranian is an avid chewer, natural bones may wear away his teeth prematurely; hence, they then should be taken away from your dog when the teething purposes have been served. The badly worn, and usually painful, teeth of many mature dogs can be traced to excessive chewing on natural bones.

THE GUIDE TO OWNING A POMERANIAN

Contrary to popular belief, knuckle bones that can be chewed up and swallowed by your Pomeranian provide little, if any, usable calcium or other nutriment. They do, however, disturb the digestion of most dogs and cause them to vomit the nourishing food they need.

Dried rawhide products of various types, shapes, sizes, and prices are available on the market and have become quite popular. However, they don't serve the primary chewing functions very well; they are a bit messy when wet from mouthing, and most Pomeranians chew them up rather rapidly—but they have been considered safe for dogs until recently. Now, more and more incidents of death, and near death, by strangulation have been reported to be the results of partially swallowed chunks of rawhide swelling in the throat. More recently, some veterinarians have been attributing cases of acute constipation to large pieces of incompletely digested rawhide in the intestine.

A new product, molded rawhide, is very safe. During the process, the rawhide is melted and then injection molded into the familiar dog shape. It is very hard and is eagerly accepted by Pomeranians. The melting process also sterilizes the rawhide. Don't confuse this with pressed rawhide, which is nothing more than small strips of rawhide squeezed together.

Through gentle tugging, Nylabone® Dental Chew Floss is highly effective in removing destructive plaque between teeth and beneath the gumline.

The nylon bones, especially those with natural meat and bone fractions added, are probably the most complete, safe, and economical answer to the chewing need. Dogs cannot break them or bite off sizable chunks; hence, they are completely safe—and being longer lasting than other things offered for the purpose, they are economical.

Hard chewing raises little bristle-like projections on the surface of the nylon bones—to provide effective interim tooth cleaning and vigorous gum massage, much in the same way your toothbrush does it for you. The little projections are raked off and swallowed in the form of thin shavings, but the chemistry of the nylon is such that they break down in the stomach fluids and pass through without effect.

The toughness of the nylon provides the strong chewing resistance needed for important jaw exercise and effectively aids teething functions, but there is no tooth wear because nylon is non-abrasive. Being inert, nylon does not support the growth of microorganisms; and it can be washed in soap and water or it can be sterilized by boiling or in an autoclave.

Nylabone® is highly recommended by veterinarians as a safe, healthy nylon bone that can't splinter or chip. Nylabone® is frizzled by the dog's chewing action, creating a toothbrush-like surface that cleanses the teeth and massages the gums. Nylabone®, the only chew products made of flavor-impregnated solid nylon, are available in your local pet shop. Nylabone® is superior to the cheaper bones because it is made of virgin nylon, which is the strongest and longest-lasting type of nylon available. The cheaper bones are made from recycled or re-ground nylon scraps, and have a tendency to break apart and split easily.

Nothing, however, substitutes for periodic professional attention for your Pomeranian's teeth and gums, not any more than your toothbrush can do that for you. Have your Pomeranian's teeth cleaned at least once a year by your veterinarian (twice a year is better) and he will be happier, healthier, and far more pleasant to live with.

Training Your Pomeranian

You owe proper training to your Pomeranian. The right and privilege of being trained is his birthright; and whether your Pomeranian is going to be a handsome, well-mannered housedog and companion, a show dog, or whatever possible use he may be put to, the basic training is

All dogs must be trained to listen to their owners. Your Pomeranian should be trained by you so that he is always attentive and obedient.

Obedience classes allow you to meet other new owners and do the training yourself under a head trainer.

always the same—all must start with basic obedience, or what might be called "manner training."

Your Pomeranian must come instantly when called and obey the "Sit" or "Down" command just as fast; he must walk quietly at "Heel," whether on or off lead. He must be mannerly and polite wherever he goes; he must be polite to strangers on the street and in stores. He must be mannerly in the presence of other dogs. He must not bark at children on roller skates, motorcycles, or other domestic animals. And he must be restrained from chasing cats. It is not a dog's inalienable right to chase

cats, and he must be reprimanded for it.

PROFESSIONAL TRAINING

How do you go about this training? Well, it's a very simple procedure, pretty well standardized by now. First, if you can afford the extra expense, you may send your Pomeranian to a professional trainer, where in 30 to 60 days he will learn how to be a "good dog." If you enlist the services of a good professional trainer, follow his advice of when to come to see the dog. No, he won't forget you, but too-frequent visits at the wrong time may slow down his training progress. And using a "pro" trainer means that you will have to go

Training your dog should be a fun experience for you and your dog. This Pom is learning the down command.

Give your Pom the proper training to prevent household accidents and mishaps.

"I passed, I passed!" This Pomeranian jumps for joy, as he is a perfectly trained dog. Finishing training procedures is very rewarding for both dog and owner.

for some training, too, after the trainer feels your Pomeranian is ready to go home. You will have to learn how your Pomeranian works, just what to expect of him and how to use what the dog has learned after he is home.

OBEDIENCE TRAINING CLASS

Another way to train your Pomeranian (many experienced Pomeranian people think this is the best) is to join an obedience training class right in your own community. There is such a group in nearly every community nowadays. Here you will be working with a group of people who are also just starting out. You will actually be training your own dog, since all work is done under the direction of a head trainer who will make suggestions to you and also tell you when and how to correct your Pomeranian's errors. Then, too, working with such a group, your Pomeranian will learn to get along with other dogs. And, what is more important, he will learn to do exactly what he is told to do, no matter how much confusion there is around him or how great the temptation is to go his own way.

Write to your national kennel club for the location of a training club or class in your locality. Sign up. Go to it regularly—every session! Go early and leave late! Both you and your Pomeranian will benefit tremendously.

TRAIN HIM BY THE BOOK

The third way of training your Pomeranian is by the book. Yes, you can do it this way and do a good job of it too. But in using the book method, select a book, buy it, study it carefully; then study it some more, until the procedures are almost second nature to you. Then start your training. But stay with the book and its advice and exercises. Don't start in and then make up a few rules of your own. If you don't follow the book, you'll get into jams you can't get out of by yourself. If after a few hours of short training sessions your Pomeranian is still not working as he should, get back to the book for a study session, because it's your fault, not the dog's! The procedures of dog training have been so well systemized that it must be your fault, since literally thousands of fine Pomeranians have been trained by the book.

After your Pomeranian is "letter perfect" under all conditions, then, if you wish, go on to advanced training and trick work.

Your Pomeranian will love his obedience training, and you'll burst with pride at the finished product! Your Pomeranian will enjoy life even more, and you'll enjoy your Pomeranian more. And remember—*you owe good training to your Pomeranian.*

Showing Your Pomeranian

A show Pomeranian is a comparatively rare thing. He is one out of several litters of puppies. He happens to be born with a degree of physical perfection that closely approximates

Your Pom needs to be properly groomed for the show ring. Don't wait until the last minute to finish grooming.

the standard by which the breed is judged in the show ring. Such a dog should, on maturity, be able to win or approach his championship in good, fast company at the larger shows. Upon finishing his championship, he is apt to be as highly desirable as a breeding animal. As a proven stud, he will automatically command a high price for service.

Showing Pomeranians is a lot of fun—yes, but it is a highly competitive sport. While all the experts were once beginners, the odds are against a novice. You will be showing against experienced handlers, often people who have devoted a lifetime to breeding, picking the right ones, and then showing those dogs through to their championships. Moreover, the most perfect Pomeranian ever born has

If you plan on showing your Pomeranian, you need to become familiar with the breed standard.

faults, and in your hands the faults will be far more evident than with the experienced handler who knows how to minimize his Pomeranian's faults. These are but a few points on the sad side of the picture.

The experienced handler, as I say, was not born knowing the ropes. He learned—and so can you! You can if you will put in the same time, study and keen observation that he did. But it will take time!

KEY TO SUCCESS

First, search for a truly fine show prospect. Take the puppy home, raise him by the book, and as carefully as you know how, give him every chance to mature into the Pomeranian you hoped for. My advice is to keep your dog out of big shows, even Puppy Classes, until he is mature. Maturity in the male is roughly two years; with the female, 14 months or so. When your Pomeranian is approaching maturity, start out at match shows, and, with this experience for both of you, then go gunning for the big wins at the big shows.

Next step, read the standard by which the Pomeranian is judged. Study it until you know it by heart. Having done this, and while your puppy is at home (where he should be) growing into a normal, healthy Pomeranian, go to every dog show you can possibly reach. Sit at the ringside and watch Pomeranian judging. Keep your ears and eyes open. Do your own judging, holding each of those dogs against the standard, which you now know by heart.

In your evaluations, don't start looking for faults. Look for the virtues—the best qualities. How does a given Pomeranian shape up against the standard? Having looked for and noted the virtues, then note the faults and see what prevents a given Pomeranian from standing correctly or moving well. Weigh these faults against the virtues, since, ideally, every feature of the dog should contribute to the harmonious whole dog.

"RINGSIDE JUDGING"

It's a good practice to make notes on each Pomeranian, always holding the dog against the standard. In "ringside judging," forget your personal preference for this or that feature. What does the standard say about it? Watch carefully as the judge places the dogs in a given class. It is difficult from the ringside always to see why number one was placed over the second dog. Try to follow the judge's reasoning. Later try to talk with the judge after he is finished. Ask him questions as to why he placed certain Pomeranians and not others. Listen while the judge explains his placings, and, I'll say right here, any judge worthy of his license should be able to give reasons.

When you're not at the ringside, talk with the fanciers and breeders who have Pomeranians. Don't be afraid to ask opinions or say that you don't know. You have a lot of listening to do, and it will help you a great deal and speed up your personal progress if you are a good listener.

THE NATIONAL CLUB

You will find it worthwhile to join the national Pomeranian club and to subscribe to its magazine. From the national club, you will learn the location of an approved regional club near you. Now, when your young Pomeranian is eight to ten months old, find out the dates of match shows in your section of the country. These differ from regular shows only in that no championship points are given. These shows are especially designed to launch young dogs (and new handlers) on a show career.

ENTER MATCH SHOWS

With the ring deportment you have

To be successful at shows, look for the good things about other Pomeranians not the bad ones. This ribbon winner has all the qualities of a first-class show dog.

watched at big shows firmly in mind and practice, enter your Pomeranian in as many match shows as you can. When in the ring, you have two jobs. One is to see to it that your Pomeranian is always being seen to its best advantage. The other job is to keep your eye on the judge to see what he may want you to do next. Watch only the judge and your Pomeranian. Be quick and be alert; do exactly as the judge directs. Don't speak to him except to answer his questions. If he does something you don't like, don't say so. And don't irritate the judge (and everybody else) by constantly talking and fussing with your dog.

In moving about the ring, remember to keep clear of dogs beside you or in front of you. It is my advice to you not to show your Pomeranian in a regular point show until he is at least close to maturity and after both you and your dog have had time to perfect ring manners and poise in the match show.

Your Pomeranian's Health

We know our pets, their moods and habits, and therefore we can recognize when our Pomeranian is experiencing an off-day. Signs of sickness can be very obvious or very subtle. As any mother can attest, diagnosing and treating an ailment require common sense, knowing when to seek home remedies and when to visit your doctor...or veterinarian, as the case may be.

Coat maintenance is very important to keep Pomeranians healthy. Grooming for good health makes good sense.

As any mother can attest, it is important to know your Pomeranian's moods and habits so you can recognize when he is not feeling well.

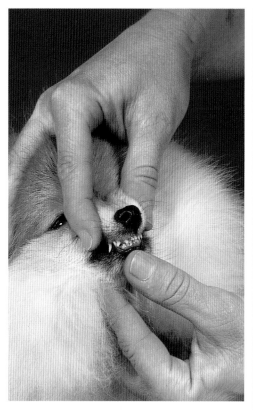
Your Pomeranian's teeth should be checked on a regular basis.

Your veterinarian, we know, is your Pomeranian's best friend, next to you. It will pay to be choosy about your veterinarian. Talk to dog-owning friends whom you respect. Visit more than one vet before you make a lifelong choice. Trust your instincts. Find a knowledgeable, compassionate vet who knows Pomeranians and likes them.

The Pomeranian's coat is long and full and at any age benefits from regular brushing to develop and keep looking its best. Brushing stimulates the natural oils in the coat and also removes dead haircoat. The Pomeranian's coat is a double coat, which means it is composed of a harsher, longer outer coat (the coat that you see) and a soft, cottony undercoat (which you don't see until your dog sheds, but gives the Pom's coat a look of fullness and density). All breeds of spitz dogs (such as Huskies and American Eskimos) have double coats, and all require considerable grooming to keep the coats glossy and clean.

The puppy coat takes about ten months to develop into the double coat and will go through three or four stages before starting to look like "the Poms in the pictures." These stages are described as long and blowy, to short and nappy, to fuzzy and unmanageable—eventually the undercoat and outer coat cooperate to create an appearance that is worthy of the Pomeranian's heritage. Yet, the adult may not have a mature double coat until it is three-and-a-half or four years of age.

Grooming for good health makes good sense. Puppies, in all these stages of "uglies" and "shabbies," require plenty of grooming to usher in the impressive and heavy adult coat. Pomeranians may be prone to skin irritations too, so grooming can help minimize any potential skin maladies.

ANAL SACS

Anal sacs, sometimes called anal glands, are located in the musculature

Keep your Pomeranian's bedding clean to prevent illness.

Tear duct abnormalities are not uncommon to Pomeranians, so keep the eyes clean and free of debris.

of the anal ring, one on either side. Each empties into the rectum via a small duct. Occasionally their secretion becomes thickened and accumulates so you can readily feel these structures from the outside. If your Pomeranian is scooting across the floor dragging his rear quarters, or licking his rear, his anal sacs may need to be expressed. Placing pressure in and up towards the anus, while holding the tail, is the general routine. Anal sac secretions are characteristically foul-smelling, and you could get squirted if not careful. Veterinarians can take care of this during regular visits and demonstrate the cleanest method.

MAJOR HEALTH ISSUES

Fortunately, the Pomeranian is among the healthiest of dogs with an expected life span of 12 to 14 years. Of course some exceptional Poms have lived to 18 or 20! Like other small dogs, Poms are prone to luxated patellas (which are loose knee caps). The combination of smallness and the delicate bones of the Pomeranian make dislocations and broken bones common injuries. Pomeranian owners should be aware that their little friends are somewhat frail and should not be mishandled or allowed to climb and jump in high places. These potential orthopedic problems, though, are not major concerns and can usually be treated by a veterinarian. Another similarity with his fellow toy breeds are low blood sugar, dwarfism, and open skulls (incomplete fusion of the bones of the head). Breeders are aware of these concerns and make conscious efforts to minimize their occurrence. Veterinarians report that Poms have been know to have hydrocephalus, hypothyroidism, kidney disease, and a lung disorder known as patent ductus arteriosus, as well as eye problems including progressive retinal atrophy, among the most common of all congenital defects in purebred dogs, and tear duct abnormalities.

When your Pom returns inside after playing outside, examine his coat for ticks or any other parasites that may transmit disease.

VACCINATIONS

For the continued health of your dog, owners must attend to vaccinations regularly. Your veterinarian can recommend a vaccination schedule appropriate for your dog, taking into consideration the factors of climate and geography. The basic vaccinations to protect your dog are: parvovirus, distemper, hepatitis, leptospirosis, adenovirus, parainfluenza, coronavirus, bordetella, tracheobronchitis (kennel cough), Lyme disease and rabies.

Parvovirus is a highly contagious, dog-specific disease, first recognized in 1978. Targeting the small intestine, parvo affects the stomach, and diarrhea and vomiting (with blood) are clinical signs. Although the dog can pass the infection to other dogs within three days of infection, the initial signs, which include lethargy and depression, don't display themselves until four to seven days. When affecting puppies under four weeks of age, the heart muscle is frequently attacked. When the heart is affected, the puppies exhibit difficulty in breathing and experience crying and foaming at the nose and mouth.

Distemper, related to human measles, is an airborne virus that spreads in the blood and ultimately in the nervous system and epithelial tissues. Young dogs or dogs with weak immune systems can develop encephalomyelitis (brain disease) from the distemper infection. Such dogs experience seizures, general

Before you bring your puppy home, he should have received at least one set of inoculations. Ask the seller of your puppy for health papers.

THE GUIDE TO OWNING A POMERANIAN

weakness and rigidity, as well as "hardpad." Since distemper is largely incurable, prevention through vaccination is vitally important. Puppies should be vaccinated at six to eight weeks of age, with boosters at 10 to 12 weeks. Older puppies (16 weeks and older) who are unvaccinated should receive no fewer than two vaccinations at three- to four-week intervals.

Hepatitis mainly affects the liver and is caused by canine adenovirus type I. Highly infectious, hepatitis often affects dogs 9 to 12 months of age. Initially the virus localizes in the dog's tonsils and then disperses to the liver, kidneys and eyes. Generally speaking the dog's immune system is capable of combating this virus. Canine infectious hepatitis affects dogs whose systems cannot fight off the adenovirus. Affected dogs have fever, abdominal pains, bruising on mucous membranes and gums, and experience coma and convulsions. Prevention of hepatitis exists only through vaccination at eight to ten weeks of age and then boosters three or four weeks later, then annually.

Leptospirosis is a bacterium-related disease often spread by rodents. The organisms that spread leptospirosis enter through the mucous membranes and spread to the internal organs via the bloodstream. It can be passed through the dog's urine. Leptospirosis does not affect

Love and companionship are keys to having a healthy Pomeranian. If properly supervised, a child can be a Pom's best friend.

young dogs as consistently as the other viruses; it is reportedly regional in distribution and somewhat dependent on the immunostatus of the dog. Fever, inappetence, vomiting, dehydration, hemorrhage, kidney and eye disease can result in moderate cases.

Bordetella, called canine cough, causes a persistent hacking cough in dogs and is very contagious. Bordetella involves a virus and a bacteria: parainfluenza is the most common virus implicated; *Bordetella bronchiseptica*, the bacterium. Bronchitis and pneumonia result in less than 20 percent of the cases, and most dogs recover from the condition within a week to four weeks. Non- prescription medicines can help relieve the hacking cough, though nothing can cure the condition before it's run its course. Vaccination cannot guarantee protection from canine cough, but it does ward off the most common virus responsible for the condition.

Lyme disease (also called borreliosis), although known for decades, was only first diagnosed in dogs in 1984. Lyme disease can affect cats, cattle, and horses, but especially people. In the US, the disease is transmitted by two ticks carrying the Borrelia burgdorferi organism: the deer tick (Ixodes scapularis) and the western black-legged tick (Ixodes pacificus), the latter primarily affects reptiles. In Europe, Ixodes ricinus is responsible for spreading Lyme. The disease causes lameness, fever, joint swelling, inappetence, and lethargy. Removal of ticks from the dog's coat can help reduce the chances of Lyme, though not as much as avoiding heavily wooded areas where the dog is most likely to contract ticks. A vaccination is available, though it has not been proven to protect dogs from all strains of the organism that cause the disease.

Rabies is passed to dogs and people through wildlife; in North America, principally through the skunk, fox and raccoon—the bat was never the culprit it was once thought to be. Likewise, the common image of the rabid dog foaming at the mouth with every hair on end is unlikely the truest scenario. A rabid dog exhibits difficulty eating, salivates much and has spells of paralysis and awkwardness. Before a dog reaches this final state, it may experience anxiety, personality changes, irritability and more aggressiveness than is usual. Vaccinations are strongly recommended as rabid dogs are too dangerous to manage and are commonly euthanized. Puppies are generally vaccinated at 12 weeks of age, and then annually. Although rabies is on the decline in the world community, tens of thousands of humans die each year from rabies-related incidents.

COPING WITH PARASITES

Parasites have clung to our pets for centuries. Despite our modern efforts, fleas still pester our pet's existence, and our own. All dogs itch, and fleas can make even the happiest dog a miserable, scabby mess. The loss of hair and habitual biting and chewing at themselves rank among the annoyances; the nuisances include the passing of tapeworms and the whole family's itching through the summer months. A full range of flea-control and elimination products are available at pet shops,

If you properly care for your Pom, he'll be happy and healthy throughout his life.

and your veterinarian surely has recommendations. Sprays, powders, collars and dips fight fleas from the outside; drops and pills fight the good fight from inside. Discuss the possibilities with your vet. Not all products can be used in conjunction with one another, and some dogs may be more sensitive to certain applications than others. The dog's living quarters must be debugged as well as the dog itself. Heavy infestation may require multiple treatments.

Always check your dog for ticks carefully. Although fleas can be acquired almost anywhere, ticks are more likely to be picked up in heavily treed areas, pastures or other outside grounds (such as dog shows or obedience trials). Athletic, active, and hunting dogs are the most likely subjects, though any passing dog can be the host. Remember Lyme disease is passed by tick infestation.

As for internal parasites, worms are potentially dangerous for dogs and people. Roundworms, hookworms, whipworms, tapeworms, and heartworms comprise the "blightsome" party of troublemakers. Deworming puppies begins at around two to three weeks and continues until three months of age. Proper hygienic care of the environment is also important to prevent contamination with roundworm and hookworm eggs. Heartworm preventatives are recom-

mended by most veterinarians, although there are some drawbacks to the regular introduction of poisons into our dogs' system. These daily or monthly preparations also help regulate most other worms as well. Discuss worming procedures with your veterinarian.

Roundworms pose a great threat to dogs and people. They are found in the intestine of dogs, and can be passed to people through ingestion of feces-contaminated dirt. Roundworm infection can be prevented by not walking dogs in heavy-traffic people areas, by burning feces, and by curbing dogs in a responsible manner. (Of course, in most areas of the country, curbing dogs is the law.) Roundworms are typically passed from the bitch to the litter, and the bitch should be treated along with the puppies, even if she tested negative prior to whelping. Generally puppies are treated every two weeks until two months of age.

Hookworms, like roundworms, are also a danger to dogs and people. The hookworm parasite (known as *Ancylostoma caninum*) causes cutaneous larva migrans in people. The eggs of hookworms are passed in feces and become infective in shady, sandy areas. The larvae penetrate the skin of the dog, and the dog subsequently becomes infected. When swallowed, these parasites affect the intestines, lungs, windpipe, and the whole digestive system. Infected dogs suffer from anemia and lose large amounts of blood in the places where the worms latch onto the dog's intestines, etc.

Although infrequently passed to humans, whipworms are cited as one of the most common parasites in America. These elongated worms affect the intestines of the dog, where they latch on, and cause colic upset or diarrhea. Unless identified in stools passed, whipworms are difficult to diagnose. Adult worms can be eliminated more consistently than the larvae, since whipworms exhibit unusual life cycles. Proper hygienic care of outdoor grounds is critical to the avoidance of these harmful parasites.

Tapeworms are carried by fleas and enter the dog when the dog swallows the flea. Humans can acquire tapeworms in the same way, though we are less likely to swallow fleas than dogs are. Recent studies have shown that certain rodents and wild animals have been infected with tapeworms, and dogs can be affected by catching and/or eating these other animals. Of course, outdoor hunting dogs and terriers are more likely to be infected in this way than are your typical house dog or non-motivated hound.

Treatment for tapeworm has proven very effective, and infected dogs do not show great discomfort or symptoms. When people are infected, however, the liver can be seriously damaged. Proper cleanliness is the best bet against tapeworms.

Heartworm disease is transmitted by mosquitoes and badly affects the lungs, heart and blood vessels of dogs. The larvae of *Dirofilaria immitis* enters the dog's bloodstream when bitten by an infected mosquito. The larvae takes about six months to mature. Infected dogs suffer from weight loss, appetite loss, chronic coughing and general fatigue. Not all affected dogs show signs of illness right away, and carrier dogs may be affected for years before clinical signs appear. Treatment of heartworm disease has been effective but can be dangerous also. Prevention as always is the desirable alternative. Ivermectin is the active ingredient in most heartworm preventatives and has proven to be successful. Check with your veterinarian for the preparation best for your dog. Dogs generally begin taking the preventatives at eight months of age and continue to do so throughout the non-winter months.

Index

Photo Credits

Denise P. Cherry, Cott/Francis Studios, Isabelle Francais, Ceila Ooi, Robert Pearcy, Vince Serbin, Robert Smith and Karen Taylor.